TWO WORKS

Michael Choniates
Archbishop of Athens

Translated by: D.P. Curtin

TWO WORKS

Copyright @ 2020 Dalcassian Press

All rights reserved. No part of this publication may be reproduced, distributed, or transmitted in any form or by any means, including photocopying, recording, or other electronic or mechanical methods, without the prior written permission of the publisher, except in the case of brief quotations embodied in critical reviews and certain other non-commercial uses permitted by copyright law. For permission request, write to Dalcassian Press at dalcassianpublishing at gmail.com

ISBN: 979-8-3302-6031-7 (Paperback)

Library of Congress Control Number:
Author: Curtin, D.P. (1985-)

Printed by Ingram Content Group, 1 Ingram Blvd, La Vergne, Tennessee

First printing edition 2020.

TWO WORKS

Sermon for Palm Sunday

The most illustrious prophet of kings, David, admiring the immense beauty of the sun, and his tireless speed, also said: "As a bridegroom coming out of his chamber, he rejoices as a strong man to run his course; his going forth is from the end of the heaven, and his circuit unto the ends of it: and there is nothing hid from the heat thereof." Indeed, this most wise man marvels at this greatest star, how it rises with such shining beauty like a bridegroom in the eastern horizon, and with giant speed and strength it reaches the opposite horizon, with no dimming of its beauty and splendor over the vast volumes of years, not being dissolved by force, but always rejoicing in the same manner, illuminating the entirety of things effortlessly, and filling everything with the most vital, sparkling light. Furthermore, I, who see the Sun of Justice, Christ, and the Creator of the stars, proceeding in a new era, am led to sing with David, namely that he, as a bridegroom coming out of his chamber, rejoices as a strong man to run his course, through the midst of Jerusalem, surpassing in appearance all triumphs and miracles of past ages, exulting in an extraordinary manner. Indeed, his course extends from the highest heaven: for the sake of your salvation, he began to make a way without being confined to a place; and his circuit reaches to the ends of the sky, even to the lowest parts of the underworld; there, the course of his dispensation had its end, so that even those infernal places were not hidden from his heat. And then, as if rising from the west, he is restored to the same seats of heaven. However, before shining among the dead in the underworld, he sent forth a divine voice, raising a certain one from the dead after four days, whose victory is celebrated today in a procession, establishing a present triumph from that time; namely, that gentle King of Zion, not adorned with golden trappings on a horse or in a golden chariot, but riding on a humble donkey. Having been carried from the county, the King of glory, having engaged in conflict against hell, approached its prey closely, and from there he brought the dearest Lazarus as a first fruit. With the sound of a single voice, he terrified the strongholds of the tyrant, and from the midst of the gaping jaws of the devouring monster, the good Shepherd rescued his sheep. The thief was holding Lazarus captured in his den; however, soon after hearing the voice of the Lord, he roared in anger and let him emerge into the breath of reviving light. For it was not right for him to sleep in death as if born from a woman, but to awaken as the dearest to life itself. Oh, the immense power, nay, the all-powerful voice! By which the gates of death are opened in fear, and the guardians of hell are astonished, and the dead man leaped out after four days. Truly Christ is the lion's cub; and now with a single roar he terrifies the wild beast: "The lion will roar," he says, "and who will not be afraid"? But shortly after, he too will lie down to rest; but when he has engaged in combat with death as if on equal footing, he will utterly defeat it. Indeed, he has subdued a fearful and immense crowd with a single cry from afar: but soon he will be swallowed willingly, like Jonah, by the gaping mouth, and with his belly torn open, he will extract all those he has swallowed from the beginning of time. Although Lazarus was on the earth and had gone into the earth, yet it was Christ who had created man from the earth; from him, with a cry as well as a breath, he poured forth life into the dead form again. Indeed, the decomposed and corrupted corpse was stinking with decay, but the voice of Christ was its life-giving fragrance. The man who was bound by the chains of death and tightly bound, he did not allow to stay close but commanded to go far away, namely Christ: "Come out, you who leads the captives in strength; likewise those who dwell in the tombs."

TWO WORKS

Let Lazarus now sing with David: "You have not abandoned my soul to the underworld, nor have you allowed your holy one to see corruption," and "You have filled me with joy with your face: for I have not been abandoned to oblivion, like one dead from the heart," but to me, who was dead, "You have done wonders". Indeed, Christ exhibited many magnificent works, by which he wanted to make his glory manifest to the Jews devoid of understanding; and he raised many dead, namely the servant of the centurion, the daughter of Jairus, the only son of the widow. Indeed, the dead, upon hearing, "Little girl, rise", and "Young man, I tell you, rise", immediately obeyed the command and saw the light of the resurrected; however, they did not even see what they were seeing, nor hear what they were hearing.

Therefore, even in the case of the resurrection of Lazarus at the end, which surpassed all other miracles in novelty, as if its power were greater, he applied a remedy. For indeed, he immediately raised those dead; but this one, when he had already begun to decay, and his elements in which the structure of the body had congealed were dissolving. There, indeed, he touched the coffin of the deceased and took the girl's hand, restoring her to life by the touch of his life-giving body; but here, he restored life by his voice alone, a voice that the Jewish people did not hear, so that death might feed on those whom, according to David, it was to feed on; which indeed, like sheep, those who labored in blindness, it would place in hell: but Lazarus, as a sheep of Christ, immediately felt the voice of the calling shepherd, and having been sent down into the abyss of hell, he returned to the one calling him. And what they indeed claimed to know about Moses, but not about the Lord, the uncircumcised asserted, he has shown more clearly today, triumphing freely, proceeding with a more royal dignity; finally, bringing forth nursing infants. So that they may acknowledge their Lord, and be witnesses, that the Lord Himself is the one who watches over the little ones, and whom David prophesied would perfect praise from the mouths of infants and nursing babies"; but Zacharias prophesied of the King of Zion, gentle and saving, who rides on a donkey." For when the Scribes and Pharisees have a veil over their hearts while the prophets and Moses are being read, and holding the key of knowledge, not only do they not enter, but they also prevent those who want to enter"; the mouths of infants, which speak of Christ, are opened up for prophesying, and those whose tongues are not used, stammering children, explain the most obscure Scriptures most clearly; they teach deaf parents, and those who block their ears like asps. "Taught by God, children, taking up the Psalms of David, and reading what is suitable and appropriate, in his songs, with the keen sight of the sun of righteousness, they clearly foresee, and for parents who do not want to see clearly, and do not renew their youth like the eagle, but are blinded by the antiquity of the scriptures, they say: Hosanna; Blessed is he who comes in the name of the Lord, King of Israel." Infants almost point with their fingers, and proclaim that the King of Zion is indeed gentle and saving. For Hosanna means the same as "Save, I pray." Nevertheless, it is not a miracle for those who are uncircumcised in heart to turn to children. They were beasts: whence neither did they enter into the kingdom of colors. For they were old and rotten wineskins and were not able to contain the grace of wine as new, and spirits capable. Oh, blindness and dullness! The ox knew his owner, and the donkey his master's crib; but Israel did not know his King, and was found more senseless than the ox, and more stupid than the donkey, in not recognizing his Lord; and this, when even the infants would not carry the ox in their tongue, but would proclaim the King riding on a donkey, and advancing in a procession today, and fulfilling what was prophesied long ago; namely, to bind his foal to the vine", that is, to gather the new people from the nations, which no one has yet subjected to the yoke, to the vine brought from Egypt".

Indeed, let us understand the power of miracles that are present in the mystery; rather, let us exhibit the wonders of celebration within ourselves. Let us become friends of Christ like Lazarus; let us make wisdom and virtue our sisters; and if it should happen that we are weakened like humans, or even fall into the sleep of death, and we are as if buried in a certain cave in the present age, Christ, who is life, will be present and will cry out with a loud voice of the great gospel teachings: "Come out from the death of this age," and as he says in another place, "Rise, let us go from here," leading us away from there and rescuing us from the death of this age; and immediately we will depart from the age, proceeding to life without any hindrance, even though it is most new and unheard of; namely, being bound by the chains of the flesh: for what binds the soul is called by the Greek word "dipas" (as if you say a chain), the body is named by the wise. However, this does not prevent us from transcending the necessity of the death of this world, as long as we hear only the voice of the Lord, and go out of the camp to him, as if we do not have a lasting city here, as the divine Apostle says, nor do we reject the hope of restoring life, even if we are infected by the desire of this world; indeed, we will have passed through the four ages - childhood, youth, manhood, and old age - and come to dissolution itself, for Christ knows how to raise the dead from sins. Let us put on the nature of the beast before the Savior, as the author David, so that we may carry him as a procession against death on our behalf. Let us strip off the garments from him, subjecting the flesh to the spirit, let us cultivate humility. If it is not yet permitted to plant trees near the outlets of water, such as a palm tree, or a cedar of Lebanon, or a fruitful olive tree (like the tree of the righteous Job, like the divine David), or branches from those holy trees, namely the shoots of virtues, from which they were bursting forth, let us remove them and come with applause to the Savior. If we are just men, truthful, without crime, worshipers of God, abstaining from all evil, we will have become like the trees of Job in a perfect manner, which indeed flourished like a lofty and leafy palm; for he said that his age would grow old, just as the trunk of a palm tree, and we will be like the fruitful olive tree of David, if we are also imitators of his strength and gentleness, so that we may be pleasing to the heart of the man, and be found by God through his ways. But if we cannot imitate all their virtues due to our sluggishness, let us at least cherish those flowers, the abundance of fruits, patience, struggles of labor, or at least the gentleness or modesty of David, by which he even called himself a worm, not a man, or peaceful manners with those who hate peace, a mind holding on to no injustices, leniency, and again the invincible constancy in temptations of Job, to free the poor from the hand of the powerful, to help the orphan who lacks assistance, to put on righteousness, and to clothe oneself in judgment as in a double garment; to be the eye of the blind, the foot of the lame, the father of the weak. If we exhibit the works of these virtues, we shall have cut enough branches from the trees by God and carried out the worship of the Savior.

Let us abstain from evil deeds: let us imitate the innocence of infants, for such is the kingdom of heaven." Even now God has perfected praise from their mouths. If you are a son of the Church, humble yourself as a weaned child with its mother. Do not cling to malice and pride, but cling to the nurse in spirit. Why do you fight against God, who rages against the bride of Christ in madness? "A curse from a mother uproots foundations." But if she is also the bride of Christ, what curse will she not fulfill? Do not, having become a son of God through baptism, be transformed into the offspring of a viper, biting and devouring the one who gave birth to you in spiritual childbirth; nor be found ungrateful, kicking against the one who has nourished you like a donkey swollen with milk. Let the whip terrify you, by which Christ today, driving out the contemptuous and those who profaned the house of prayer, expelled them by beating. Let the rope of the traitor terrify you, lest you fall into it yourself, who betrayed the master for the sake of a little money; and do not become a partner in their wicked plan, with whom it is fitting to strike the shepherd and scatter the sheep, as with Caiaphas and Pilate. For now I refrain from speaking about Korah, Dathan, and Abiram, whose rebellious assembly against Aaron, when the earth opened up and swallowed them and their families alive into hell. Nor will I mention Samuel, whose rejection God took upon himself. "They have not rejected you," he says, "but me." But we are neither Samuel, nor Elijah, nor Aaron, who called upon the Lord, and he listened to them, in the pillar of cloud. He was speaking to them: "We are not gods like them, nor sons of the Most High; but we die as men, and fall like one of the princes. Truly, you accuse us rightly, my good man," he said, "and indeed we are such; but where did this new Daniel suddenly arise for us? Who gave you the priesthood, that you may set judgment for judges, and enlighten the eye that you may extend a foot, or hand, or ear, and feed and rule the sheep as a shepherd, and make disciples as a teacher? Whose mouths of lions have you restrained? Whose dragon's belly have you torn apart without a stone or club? What future mysteries have been revealed to you? Oh, the blindness in which you see a splinter in your brother's eye, and do not notice the great beam in yourself! We are not Samuel or Aaron; for we do not keep the testimonies of God like they did, and the commandments of God which he gave us: nevertheless, just because you do not scorn those who are not judges or otherwise justify yourself, or, more wretchedly, you will be immune from punishment, partly as Christ teaches you to follow what the priests say, and not to inquire too curiously into what they do; partly as Paul advises you to obey those in authority, and be subject to them; for they watch over our souls as those who will give an account. You see, I myself am commanded to watch over you and to scrutinize diligently those things that concern you, as one who will give an account for you; I am not commanded to carry out the same roles in myself. It is prescribed to me to examine the leprosy of the people, and to declare whether one who suffers from this ailment is clean or unclean. Therefore, show respect for his dignity and reverence, by which he may be considered more venerable than the priesthood and order of Aaron and Samuel. They served the shadows of things to come, but we are clothed with the anointing of Christ's priesthood. Who should be held in greater abomination than Caiaphas, who condemned Christ? Nevertheless, such a one acts as a high priest of that year's prophecy, and that tongue, which condemned Christ to death, yields to the Spirit. Thus, God knows how to honor the priesthood, so that even for its sake, He breathes upon those who are impious with the Spirit. But you, when it is fitting for you to revere the priesthood, should be more lenient towards our weakness.

Otherwise, you presume upon what is forbidden and insult those young boys who mocked Elisha's bald head, not knowing how that head was adorned with the gifts of the Spirit. Therefore, be careful not to become prey to wild beasts and be taught not to mock a prophet, who may be bald and hairless; lacking the hair of youth, but to honor and respect what is anointed by the Spirit, just as the ointment that descended onto Aaron's head and onto that venerable beard. These things have been said by me for the sake of paternal care and discipline, not out of a desire to rebuke or seek revenge. For the injury of a brother does not have so much power as to completely vanquish Christ. Let patience explode, for which no other reason exists for the celebrations we now perform, than that long patience and gentleness of Christ, which not only endures, but also bears with undisturbed strength the most shameful spitting, beatings, slaps, and even God and the Father, for those who he calls upon them, let him reconcile all things and bring them together in the bond of unity, uniting us in one spirit and one mind, leading us to think and speak the same thing according to Christ. To him be glory forever and ever. Amen.

Letters to Eustathius, Archbishop of Thessalonica

I. *To Archbishop Eustathius of Thessalonica.*

Oh, wretched me, how much time has passed since I have not received a letter from your holiness, which would inform me about your journey and arrival in the city of Thessalonica. Perhaps now the city, newly wedded to you, like jealous women, does not allow you to set your eyes on Queen Constantine, let alone send her tokens of affection dedicated solely to her? Is it not so? But she complains of your faithlessness; she accuses you of inconsistency in love. In which she is mistaken, by your sacred head! Meanwhile, your friends are suffering from your absence; they strive to regain you, taken away from their eyes. Thus, just as the sun, just as health, is greatly valued when harsh winter, illness, or any other evil has broken out. Thus, the Athenians slandered Socrates as long as he lived among them; after drinking poison and dying, they raised his wisdom to the heavens, and they never stopped desiring the man they had previously despised from the depths of their hearts. We also feel that the love we have always embraced for you is constantly growing within us. Therefore, most wise man, since you see yourself so beloved, finally write back to us. Spare, I beg you, my ears that are surrounded by the clamors of those who inquire about your well-being. May God protect you for many years!

II. To Lord Eustathius, Archbishop of Thessalonica.
Fortunatus is a man among all. For before it was granted to him to live with your holiness, now, however, after he had been deprived of the venerable sight of your face for some time, the fortune thus willing, he has obtained the opportunity to see you again, as a traveler in the shade of a beech tree seeks rest during the summer heat. But we, troubled by the desire for you, are now deprived of all solace, since you, with whom we rejoiced in the same breeze, dwell in beloved Thessalonica, no longer offering us any comfort. To whom, if not to us, oppressed by calamities are any consoling words for the wretched? What region, if not ours burning with fire, is more plagued by flames than Thessalonica? Completely melted by excessive heat, we will be reduced to ashes when we are beyond reach in your letters. Oh, wretched me! Although the Euxine Sea sends a joyful north wind, refreshing the whole region, my soul, however, is devoured by an unquenchable fire due to your absence. Believe me, whenever I desire to ease my mind weighed down by sorrow, whenever I want to talk with a friend about those things that I do not understand well while reading, I seek them in my surroundings, but in vain. So what then? I turn my eyes to the great shepherd of Thessalonica, and I invoke with

confidence the spiritual Father, the consoler, the counselor, the helper in all things. From there, the smoke of sighs ascending from my heart accuses the burning fire within, which is somewhat alleviated by your letters for a while, but never completely extinguished. If someone were to arrange these letters in order, they would build the same steps through which you deign to descend to console us; you, I say, who exercise the greatest virtues at all times; therefore, if you are not to be counted among the choir of angels, at least you should be considered somewhat inferior to them, since you ascend and descend the same ladder with them. On the other hand, despairing about my own affairs, I feared that I would be snatched away from Providence's sight, ignorant that you were assigned to me as a faithful guardian angel, who not only as before, administered my affairs, showed the way in letters, provided everything necessary for worship, and whatever was needed. Finally, not considering the reason of time or space, the longing for you renews itself in us, like a divine book where our names are mentioned. Thessalonians, may the light shine brightly for itself and may it impart its light to us through the nightly battles of this life.

III. To Lord Archbishop Eustathius of Thessalonica.

I extol you with the highest praises, most holy lord, because you supported me when I was wavering with my hands so that I would not fall, or lifted me up when I stumbled, just as someone seizes a boy who can barely swim, or not even that, with his hands and lifts him above the waters so that he is not swallowed by the waves. Indeed, if I emerged from the abyss of things to drink the brackish water of cowardice, I still could not find the shores of life. But you, the precious good sent from heaven, the eye of Christ illuminating where I was, in what state I was, you presented a saving letter; and immediately the one who had stumbled was lifted up, and the one who was almost swallowed by the waves was held back with a strong hand. Indeed, I did not see the veil that, spread out in a wonderful way, helped Ulysses, tossed by the waves of the sea, with his limbs. Your letters, which were worn like a breastplate, was a blessing to me in saving me, especially at a time when you were not at all idle. Indeed, I never suspected that a man of letters like you would bring us the writings of Ethicus, whom I compare to Moses, who broke through the darkness with a face like a shadow, and just as Moses carried divine tablets, you carried divine letters. Did he see a burning bush while wandering in the mountains that burned his hands? As long as you bring us your successful letters, we honor you as a messenger of light and a son of the day, even though you may have dark skin. But you must continue to help as a father and a teacher to all who are found in error regarding virtue. The stronghold that the enemy nearby had built against us has been destroyed, and we have escaped the cawing nest of the jackdaws. I do not know if anything else needs to be done. Indeed, I mourn that old man who unknowingly prepared his own death, while he tried to build windy and airy houses next to his neighbor. I have not yet tasted your prayer of fasting, and I have barely begun the Monadian, like someone who removes a tablet filled with sumptuous food before you can touch it, and deceives you with false dishes, and finally deceives you. May God grant you a long life!

IV. To the same Archbishop of Thessalonica.
Behold again a man burdened with the vapors of letters, you will say, seeing our messenger, and with all right. For whatever we write is a mere vapor, and at the same time an indication of our burning love. If you love him because he comes from the city that has imbued you with letters, tell us; for it is a pleasure to us. Vapor is something that does not cease to exist, therefore even he who carries it is black like an ink-maker. However that may be, when he returns to us, he appears white and splendid in our sight after having beheld your face and having been girded with your epistolary zone. By inquiring from him, your holiness will learn how we ourselves are faring. May the Lord be propitious to me, hearing your prayers!

V. Lord Eustathius, Archbishop of Thessalonica.
Most Holy Lord, I know well that your pure soul always follows what is good and right, and that you always embrace us with the same love. You have never strayed from honorable pursuits, but have always followed their paths. The exchange of letters among friends hardly moves you, as you draw only from the soul the pledge and certainty of love. I also know that you hold our affairs dear due to your kindness, and that you continuously embrace and cherish us with love. If you love me in return, I am not like you; for the tax collectors, how can it be a matter of great importance? I wish health and longevity to those who love me with the same affection. The present monk is the brother of the venerable Demetrius of Thessaly, who is of a more timid nature, and he needs your help. Therefore, may he enjoy your kindness and paternal grace. May God be propitious to me for your sacred prayers.

VI. To Lord Eustathius, Archbishop of Thessalonica.

I wish to be with you, most sacred lord, to share in your sorrow, and to sing with Jeremiah or even our Ezekiel, because your city, the same as the once holy city, is being overwhelmed by calamity. But since we are separated at this time, I send you these letters as witnesses of my grief. What a city has been captured by enemies! Indeed, the first after the first and true queen, how much misfortune the sun of the Romans saw! Alas, the destructive force of Italian arms! How many ships with their sailors the Sicilian sea swallowed up! How the city was flooded! Woe to the Telchines! Alas, the envy that creeps upon the city's prosperity on land and sea, destroying it completely from both sides. Whose city, guilty of crime, could not be saved by the prayers of urban protectors, venerable archbishops, or all the prayers of the pious? For who would not have made devout prayers for Thessalonica, not having shared in their common hospitality? Our prayers were in vain; for God offered a cup of bitterness to be drank by all, and destroyed the luxurious city. Who, arriving in Thessalonica or Byzantium or departing for any place, was not welcomed with hospitality? The city, which was like the heart of the empire, to be preferred to Byzantium alone, to be equal in many things, now lies stricken by a common calamity. It is not surprising, most holy one, that you have suffered more than others. For God, who measures the strength of all, imposes a burden equal to each, and while sparing those who are unable to bear anything due to effeminacy, presents the most severe dangers to the bravest, to whom you seem to be numbered. Therefore, it would be absurd for a man to seek consolation who teaches us all wisdom, and whom God preserves for many years.

The Scriptorium Project is the work of a small group of lay people of various apostolic churches who are interested in the preservation, transmission, and translation of the works of the early and medieval church. Our efforts are to make the works of the church fathers accessible to anyone who might have an interest in Christian antiquities and the theological, philosophical, and moral writings that have become the bedrock of Western Civilization.

To-date, our releases have pulled from the Greek, Syriac, Georgian, Latin, Celtic, Ethiopian, and Coptic traditions of Christianity, and have been pulled from sundry local traditions and languages.

www.ingramcontent.com/pod-product-compliance
Lightning Source LLC
LaVergne TN
LVHW052049070526
838201LV00086B/5186